© 2023 Quarto Publishing Group USA Inc.
Text © Michael Bright 2023
Illustrations © Nic Jones 2023

First published in 2023 by words & pictures,
an imprint of The Quarto Group.
100 Cummings Center,
Suite 265D Beverly,
MA 01915, USA.
T (978) 282-9590 F (978) 283-2742
www.quarto.com

Editor: Kathleen Steeden
Assistant Editor: Alice Hobbs
Designer: Karen Hood
Art Director: Susi Martin
Associate Publisher: Holly Willsher

A CIP record for this book is available from
the Library of Congress.

ISBN: 978-0-7112-8352-7

9 8 7 6 5 4 3 2 1

Manufactured in Guangdong, China TT052023

MIX
Paper | Supporting
responsible forestry
FSC® C016973
FSC
www.fsc.org

words&pictures

CONTENTS

NIGHTTIME ANIMALS

Animals that are active at night are said to be nocturnal. They sleep, rest, or hide during the day. Nocturnal animals are active when daytime predators are asleep, so they only have to listen out for those that are hunting at night.

Softly, softly

While insects and frogs are especially noisy at night, many nocturnal predators are extremely quiet. Barn owls have special feathers that enable them to fly silently, so they don't alert their prey. They have a face shaped like a curved sound detector to pick up the quietest sounds of small animals, such as mice, scuttling in the undergrowth.

Listen for the echoes

The sense of hearing is important to night-flying, insect-eating bats. In the dark, they use a system called echolocation to find their way around and to home in on prey, such as nocturnal moths. The bat effectively "shouts" with high-pitched sounds. These bounce off objects ahead of the bat and its ears pick up the echoes. From these signals, its brain is able to figure out where obstacles, such as trees and buildings, are located and where prey is moving. Unlike big-eyed animals of the night, the bat can do this in complete darkness.

Hearing and smell

Nocturnal animals have well-developed senses of smell and hearing, and many rely less on sight. The bat-eared fox, for example, has large ears for picking up the very quiet sounds of the termites on which it feeds. Hedgehogs use their sharp sense of smell and a long snout to sniff out the night-active worms, slugs, snails, and insects they eat.

Nighttime eyes

At night, vision can still be a useful sense. Some animals, such as tarsiers and lorises, have enormous eyes that detect the tiniest amounts of light, like that coming from the stars. Nocturnal animals with backbones have mainly rods and few cones in the retina at the back of the eye. This enables them to see better images in dim light than diurnal animals, but their color vision is not as good.

Slits or circles

If nocturnal animals are active during the day, their pupils are often slit-shaped, like those of a cat, to prevent too much light entering the eyes and blinding them. Their pupils become round at night, especially if they are alert and about to pounce on something.

Slit-shaped pupils in day time

Round pupils at night

Night scents

Flowers that open during the night emit strong perfumes to attract night-flyers, such as moths and nectar-feeding bats. In the dark, these animals use their sense of smell to find the most fragrant blooms containing the most delicious nectar.

SOUTH AMERICAN RAIN FOREST

At night, the Amazon rain forest is hot, damp, and surprisingly noisy. There is a background hum of millions of tropical cicadas and the high-pitched croaks of tree frogs, both species trying to impress a potential partner. Piercing the air in a series of explosive blasts is the shrill call of the tree-dwelling Amazon bamboo rat "yelling" at its neighbors, so it can be heard above the racket of nighttime calls. In the dark, sound is a not only a good way for nocturnal animals to communicate with each other, but also a way in which the forest can talk to us and tell us which types of animals are there and which ones are missing, revealing whether the jungle is healthy or not.

Cicada

Night hunter

Most cats are night hunters, and in the Amazon the most formidable is the jaguar. Like all cats, its eyes are adapted for night vision with a layer of tiny mirrors (tapetum) at the backs of its eyes. These mirrors reflect light onto the light-sensitive cells (the retina), doubling the jaguar's ability to see in low light. This is the cause of "eye glow" in cats. The jaguar also has more light-sensitive cells (rods) than color-sensitive cells (cones) in its eyes, so it can see six times better than we can at night but sees less detail and color during the day.

Tree frog

Hide and seek

Up in the trees, owl monkeys are unusual, as they are active at night. Most of the other monkeys, including the uakaris, sleep high in the treetops to avoid predators, but even up here, there are killers afoot. When foraging for fruit at night, the owl monkeys must be wary of small spotted cats, like ocelots and margays, both night hunters in the canopy. The smaller margay is a skillful climber. It can turn its ankles through 180 degrees, so it can grasp branches equally well with its fore and hind paws. This means it can climb headfirst either up or down.

Giant snake

Lurking in the Amazon's rivers is the world's heaviest snake—the green anaconda. It can grow to over 17 feet long and weigh more than the average adult human. It emerges from the water, grabs its prey in its mouth and then coils its body around the victim, squeezing them to death. The snake's jaws can open so wide that it can swallow a capybara whole. It might even tackle a tapir at a clay lick.

Amazon bamboo rat

Flexible nose

The Brazilian tapir is the largest land-living animal in the Amazon. It uses its long, mobile snout to gather leaves, twigs, and fruits while foraging on the forest floor. It also visits clay licks at night. The tapir is a good swimmer, and, if threatened by danger, such as a hunting jaguar, it can dive into the river and swim to safety—but it must watch out for black caimans and anacondas.

Tarantula

AFRICAN SAVANNA

The savanna is a place of "big skies," and on a cloudless night with no Moon in sight, you can see the Milky Way in all its glory. On such nights, many of the nocturnal animals rely on starlight to navigate. Animals with eyes that see lots of detail, as ours can, are able to distinguish individual stars, so they can keep a star map in their head. Birds such as swifts and swallows, migrating to and from Africa, use the stars at night to find their way between summer breeding sites in Europe and their winter feeding sites in Africa.

Rhino rally

The black rhinoceros was always assumed to be a solitary beast, but special cameras, which can see animals lit only by the light from stars, have revealed that they meet up at waterholes at night. They are like social clubs for rhinos, places where they hang out together and get to know each other's babies, so in the future the youngsters are known to be members of the club.

Poo beetles

Little dung beetles fly at night in search of fresh piles of dung. The beetle uses the light from the Milky Way to find its way around. It does not look for the patterns of stars, since its brain is too small to take those in. Instead, it recognizes different areas of brightness in the night sky. That way it can roll its dung to a safe place where another beetle cannot steal it.

Pangolin

Aardvark

Ant-eaters

On the savanna floor, aardvarks and pangolins seek out termite mounds and ants' nests at night. Both have effective defenses against night predators, such as leopards. The aardvark has lethal claws and, if attacked, it will lie on its back and lash out with all four claws. The pangolin is more passive. It is covered in tough scales and can roll up into a ball to protect its vulnerable underside.

Lions at night

Lions hunt day and night. They have the same night vision as other cats, with the addition of a white stripe underneath each eye that reflects in even more of any available light, even if it is very dim. Like us, they cannot see if there is no light at all, but even the glow from the stars is enough for them to spot an animal worth ambushing.

Silent hunter

Baboons sleep in trees or on ledges on vertical cliff faces, safe from leopards. Leopards hunt night and day, but are really specialized to hunt at night, relying on stealth to surprise their prey. They will even jump down on an animal passing beneath a tree. Baboons are not their preferred prey because they fight back, so small antelope and smaller species of monkeys are their usual targets.

NORTH AMERICAN PRAIRIES

Many of the smaller animals of the prairies hide underground during the day and are active at night. Because the land is so flat, they would be easy to spot during the day, so they disappear below ground until it is safe to come out. At night, they can emerge from their burrows and tunnels and move around more freely at the surface, when darkness conceals their whereabouts from predators.

Great horned owl

Eerie call

One of North America's birds of the night is the whip-poor-will, a member of the nightjar family. During the day, it is so well camouflaged that it is almost invisible on the ground or lying along a branch, but at night it forages for insects. In the breeding season, it makes its eerie "whip-poor-will" call, which it repeats up to 400 times without stopping.

Bad smell

Another nighttime forager is the skunk. It repels attacks from ground-dwelling predators with the repulsive smelly liquid it squirts from its rear end, but it is still vulnerable to great horned owls that swoop in from above.

Clever mimic

In summer, when the weather is hot, prairie rattlesnakes hunt at night. They slide through the grass and slither through prairie dog tunnels in search of small rodents. Burrowing owls also take over old tunnels for their own nest sites and, if threatened by danger, such as a badger or ferret, they behave like a rattlesnake. The birds make hissing and rattling sounds, just like the snake, to frighten away the intruders.

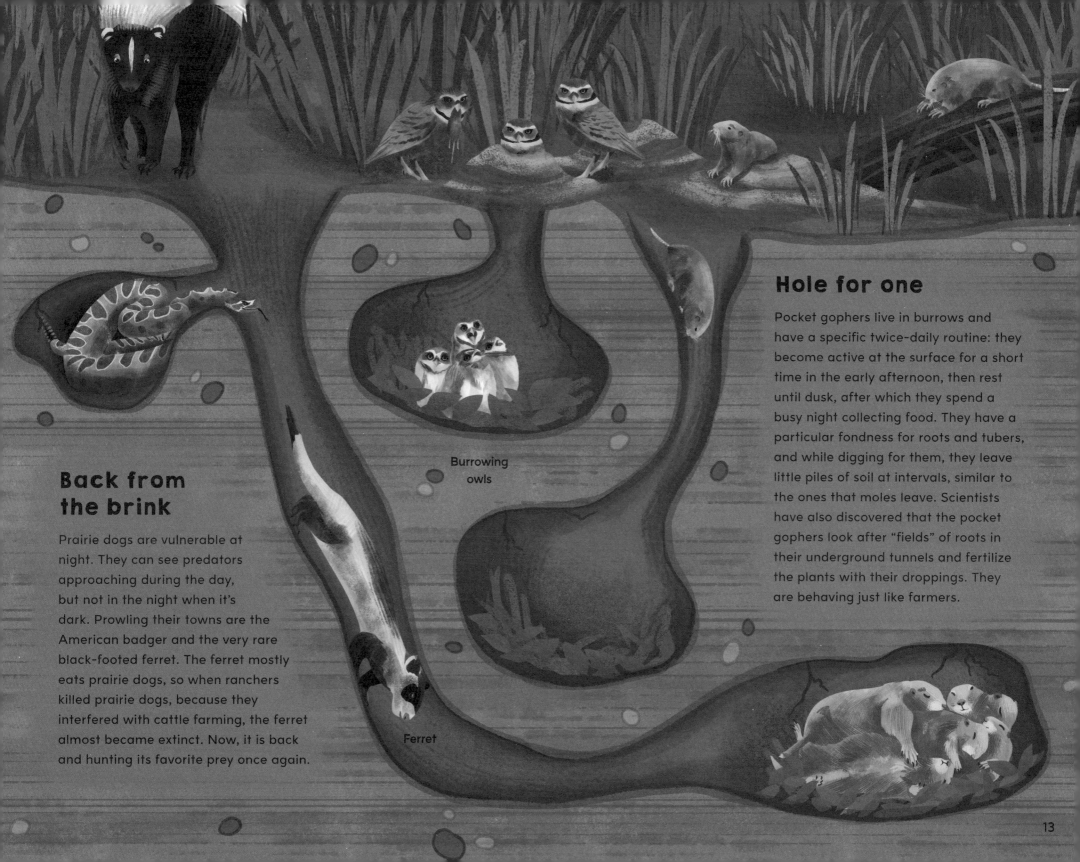

Hole for one

Pocket gophers live in burrows and have a specific twice-daily routine: they become active at the surface for a short time in the early afternoon, then rest until dusk, after which they spend a busy night collecting food. They have a particular fondness for roots and tubers, and while digging for them, they leave little piles of soil at intervals, similar to the ones that moles leave. Scientists have also discovered that the pocket gophers look after "fields" of roots in their underground tunnels and fertilize the plants with their droppings. They are behaving just like farmers.

Burrowing owls

Back from the brink

Prairie dogs are vulnerable at night. They can see predators approaching during the day, but not in the night when it's dark. Prowling their towns are the American badger and the very rare black-footed ferret. The ferret mostly eats prairie dogs, so when ranchers killed prairie dogs, because they interfered with cattle farming, the ferret almost became extinct. Now, it is back and hunting its favorite prey once again.

Ferret

13

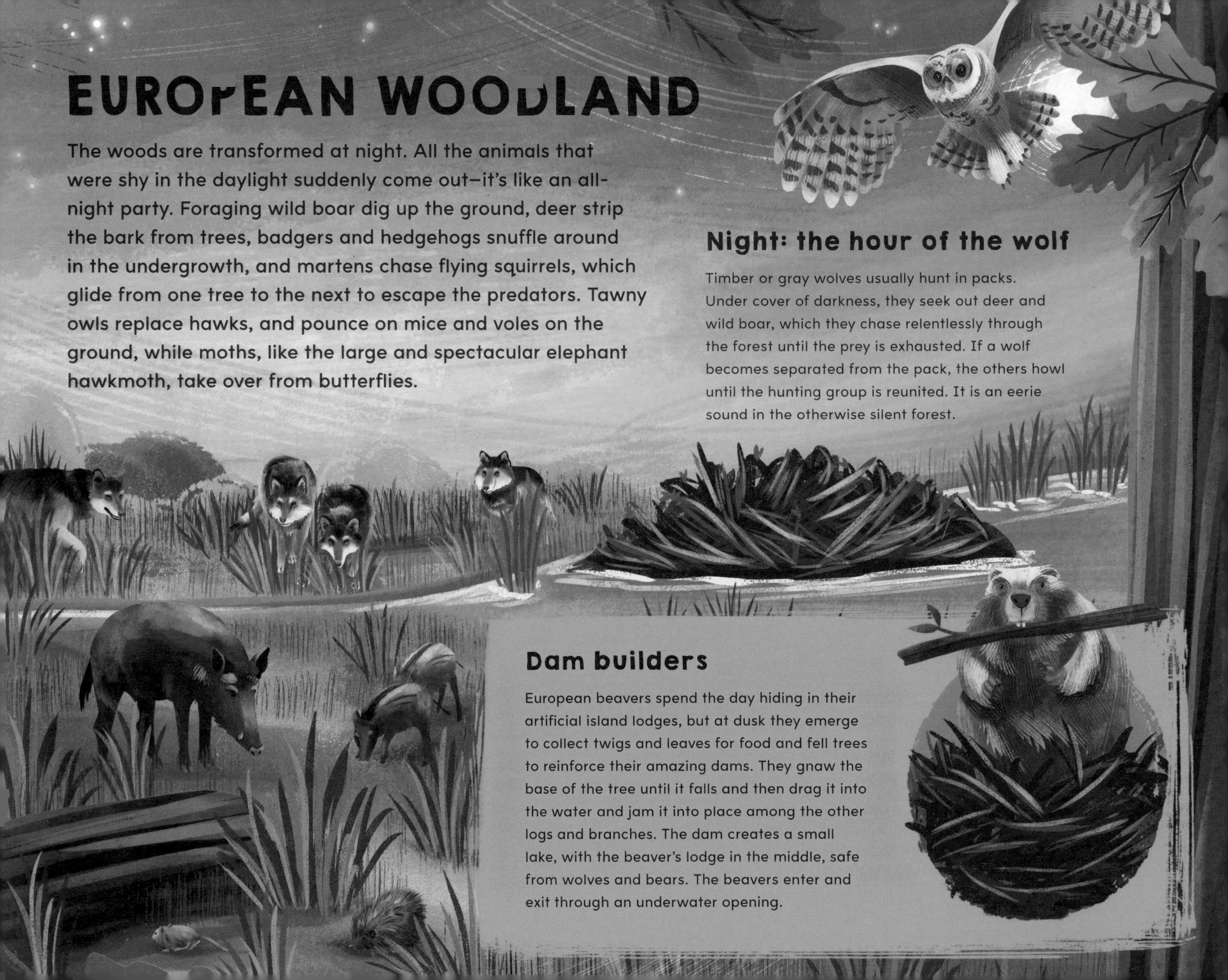

EUROPEAN WOODLAND

The woods are transformed at night. All the animals that were shy in the daylight suddenly come out—it's like an all-night party. Foraging wild boar dig up the ground, deer strip the bark from trees, badgers and hedgehogs snuffle around in the undergrowth, and martens chase flying squirrels, which glide from one tree to the next to escape the predators. Tawny owls replace hawks, and pounce on mice and voles on the ground, while moths, like the large and spectacular elephant hawkmoth, take over from butterflies.

Night: the hour of the wolf

Timber or gray wolves usually hunt in packs. Under cover of darkness, they seek out deer and wild boar, which they chase relentlessly through the forest until the prey is exhausted. If a wolf becomes separated from the pack, the others howl until the hunting group is reunited. It is an eerie sound in the otherwise silent forest.

Dam builders

European beavers spend the day hiding in their artificial island lodges, but at dusk they emerge to collect twigs and leaves for food and fell trees to reinforce their amazing dams. They gnaw the base of the tree until it falls and then drag it into the water and jam it into place among the other logs and branches. The dam creates a small lake, with the beaver's lodge in the middle, safe from wolves and bears. The beavers enter and exit through an underwater opening.

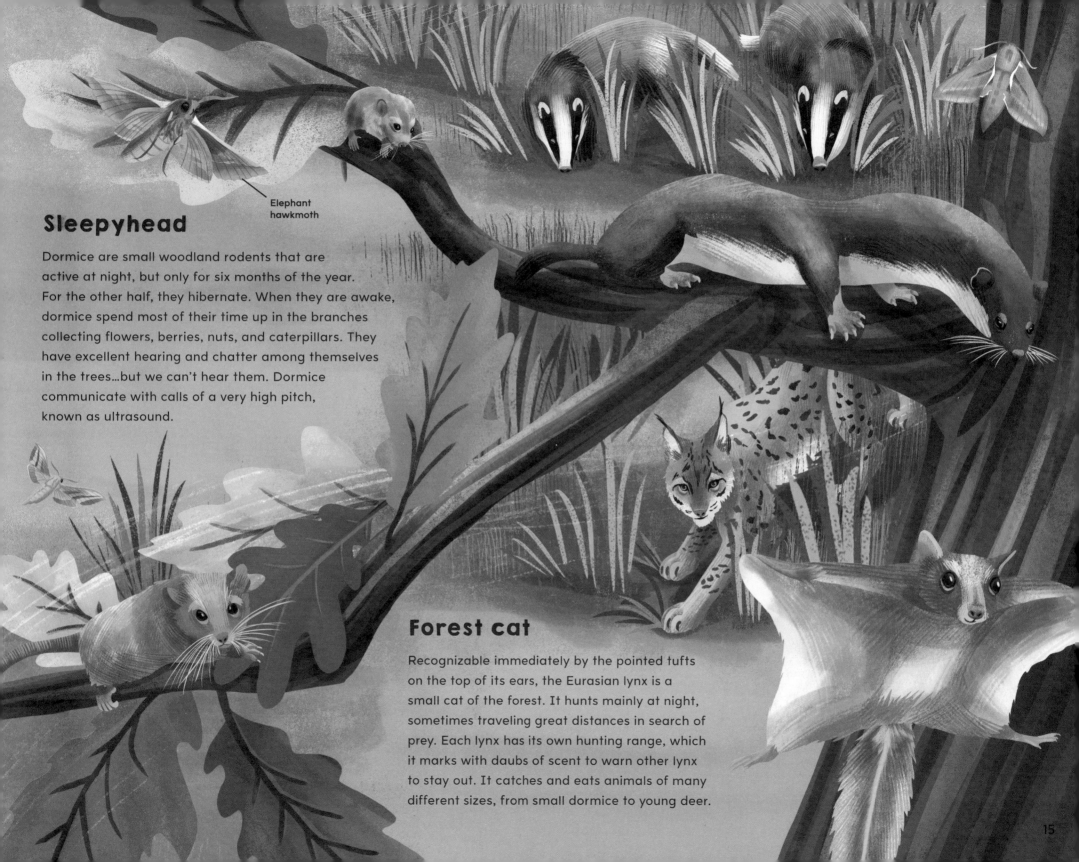

Sleepyhead

Dormice are small woodland rodents that are active at night, but only for six months of the year. For the other half, they hibernate. When they are awake, dormice spend most of their time up in the branches collecting flowers, berries, nuts, and caterpillars. They have excellent hearing and chatter among themselves in the trees...but we can't hear them. Dormice communicate with calls of a very high pitch, known as ultrasound.

Elephant hawkmoth

Forest cat

Recognizable immediately by the pointed tufts on the top of its ears, the Eurasian lynx is a small cat of the forest. It hunts mainly at night, sometimes traveling great distances in search of prey. Each lynx has its own hunting range, which it marks with daubs of scent to warn other lynx to stay out. It catches and eats animals of many different sizes, from small dormice to young deer.

SAHARA DESERT

Surprisingly, the Saharan night can be very chilly, with the temperature sometimes dropping below freezing. There are two reasons: first, the desert sand rapidly loses the heat that it gained during the day; and second, the air is so dry that there is no moisture and there are no clouds in the sky to keep the heat in, so it is lost until sunrise. With cooler temperatures, the desert really comes to life. Large animals, like the addax and dorcas gazelle, stir from their daytime resting places and feed on whatever shrubs and grasses they can find. Most of the animals, however, are much smaller. They hide in their burrows during the day, and when they emerge to feed at night, they can find warm rocks to help take away the chill if they need to.

Flying migrants

Many birds on migration, such as the reed warbler and whitethroat, stop at oases in the desert to break up their long journeys. The birds settle down during the day, and then fly on again at night. Those that fed well before they set off—and so have plenty of energy—tend to take off again the next night, while those with less fuel stick around for a few days to fatten up before heading off on the next leg of their journey.

Big ears

The fennec fox is the world's smallest type of fox. It uses its enormous ears to help it locate animals underground. The ears also act like radiators, through which the fox can lose heat when it needs to cool down. It eats both plants and animals so, like the more familiar red fox, it is an omnivore.

Reed warbler

Whitethroat

Deadly venoms

Several desert predators inject deadly venom through a sting or bite. The aptly named deathstalker scorpion has venom that could kill a human child, but its normal prey is crickets and locusts. The desert horned viper, recognised by the tiny "horns" above its eyes, is an ambush predator. It buries itself in the sand with just its eyes protruding and grabs any unsuspecting prey that wanders too close, injecting venom that causes internal bleeding. Less than 0.002 ounces of the venom is enough to kill an adult human.

Flic-flac spider

The cartwheeling flic-flac spider hunts for moths before sunrise. If it is caught out in the open and threatened by a predator itself, the spider can use its back legs to help it cartwheel away to safety. There are several desert spiders that use gravity to roll away from attackers, but this spider is the only one that can roll uphill.

Deathstalker scorpion

Predator and prey

The Saharan striped polecat lives at the edge of the desert and hunts small mammals. One of its targets is the jerboa, a rodent with big ears, which help it hear predators approaching, and long back legs that enable it to hop away from danger at speeds of up to 15 miles per hour.

SOUTHEAST ASIA CAVES AND FORESTS

In the darkness of the cave, there is the overwhelming stench of ammonia. It comes from the huge piles of bat droppings that have built up over hundreds of years on the cave floor beneath the bat roosts. The surface seethes with millions of cockroaches and darkling beetles that feast on the bat poo, and wherever there is water in the cave, freshwater crabs can be found foraging for any edible debris. All this life is dependent on the bats and birds feeding in the forest and then returning to roost or nest in the cave, where their droppings are food for the extraordinary number of animals who live inside.

Bat exit

At dusk, the cave swiftlets return to their nests and must risk being caught again. The bat hawks, though, are more focused on the animals heading out on the night shift. Streams of wrinkle-lipped bats pour out of the cave entrance and disperse throughout the forest. While the swiftlets caught the day-flying insects, the bats hunt those that fly at night.

Big eyes

In the forest canopy, the monkeys and apes are sleeping, and they are replaced by other primates. The slow loris feeds on sap and nectar. It uses its teeth to gouge out wounds in tree bark, and the noise it makes can be heard from 33 feet away. Another nocturnal primate is the monkey-like tarsier. It has huge eyes, an adaptation for hunting at night. It catches insects, such as cockroaches and grasshoppers, by leaping on them.

Silent assassin

All the smaller forest animals can fall prey to the clouded leopard, a forest cat that is just as at home in the trees as on the ground. It can even walk along a branch upside-down. It is a medium-sized cat, but it has the largest canine teeth (fangs), for its size, of any cat—they're 2 inches long. Little is known about its everyday life, because the clouded leopard is extremely rare and highly secretive.

Bat poo insects

There are so many millions of cockroaches on the surface of the bat poo that it becomes a writhing mass of yuckiness.

Mystery travelers

Bearded pigs regularly go on long migrations through the forest at night, but we don't know why they do this. A herd is led by old boars (males), and they travel along wide paths, disappearing into thickets to hide at dawn.

AN ISLAND APART: MADAGASCAR

After dark, a whole new cast of characters emerge from their daytime resting places and take to the Madagascan stage. Lemurs of one kind or another are active both during the day and at night, each species having its preferred time slot. At dusk, the diurnal lemurs usually go to bed. The nocturnal lemurs, meanwhile, wake up, and there are many different types…

Long-fingered lemur

The strangest lemur must be the aye-aye. It has large yellow eyes and big black ears, but its strangest features are on its hands. The aye-aye has unusually long fingers, which it taps on hollow logs to check if there are grubs inside. If there are, the lemur uses its extra-long middle finger to extract them.

Leaf mimic

The satanic leaf-tailed gecko looks to all the world like a leaf. It is one of several Madagascan reptiles that look just like leaves or bark. As long as they stay still, they are practically invisible during the day. Any movement would give them away, but under the cover of darkness there's a chance no one will notice, so that's when the geckos and other small lizards go in search of food.

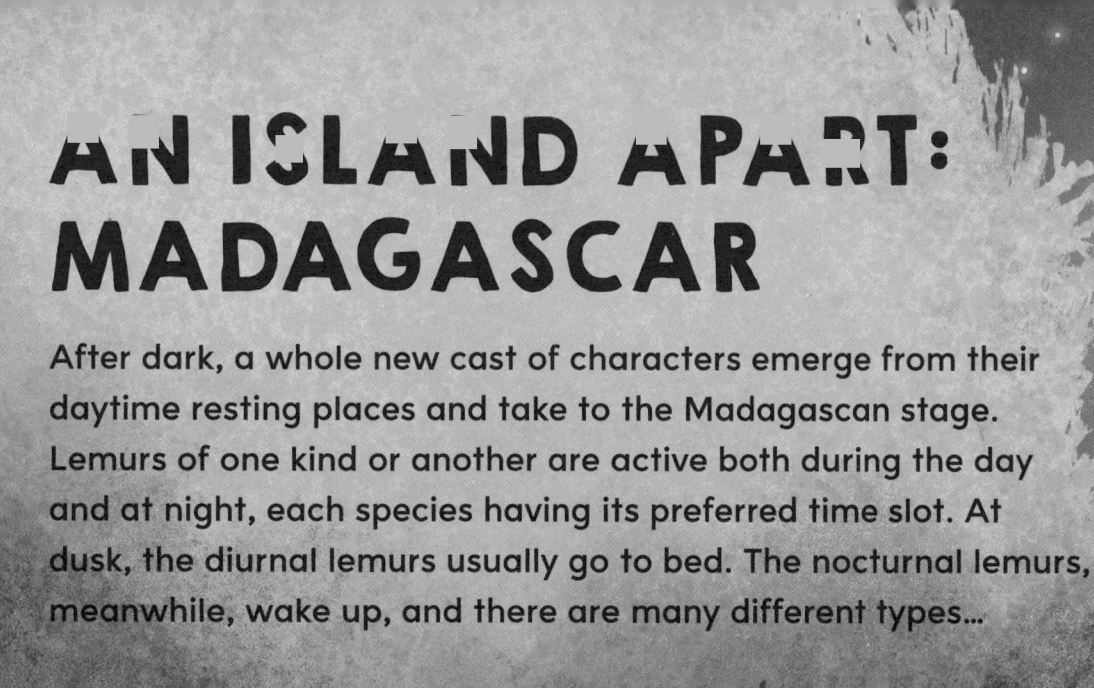

Prickly mammal

The tenrec looks like a hedgehog but it's not a hedgehog. It belongs to a completely different group of animals. Its closest relative is the African otter shrew. The tenrec has poor eyesight but extremely sensitive whiskers. Its back is covered with spines, offering protection from the fossa, which might also hunt late into the night. If attacked, the tenrec rolls into a ball with its spines facing outward, like a hedgehog. That way it protects its more vulnerable underside.

Sportive lemur

Dwarf lemur

Spectacular moth

Only the caterpillars of the adult comet moth feed—the male and female adults don't eat anything at all. They only live for four or five days, during which time they must find a mate, and the female must lay eggs before she dies.

Nighttime lemurs

Woolly lemurs live in pairs. They rest a lot, because they eat leaves, which take longer to digest than other foods, like fruit or insects. Sportive lemurs are solitary. They are highly mobile in the trees and have powerful back legs to jump between branches. Dwarf lemurs have long periods during the winter when they are not active at all. During these times, they rely on fats stored in their tails to survive.

Woolly lemurs

Dangerous frog

When caught, the bright red tomato frog puffs up and releases a substance from its skin that numbs the mouth and eyes of the predator. The attacker usually drops the frog, allowing it to escape.

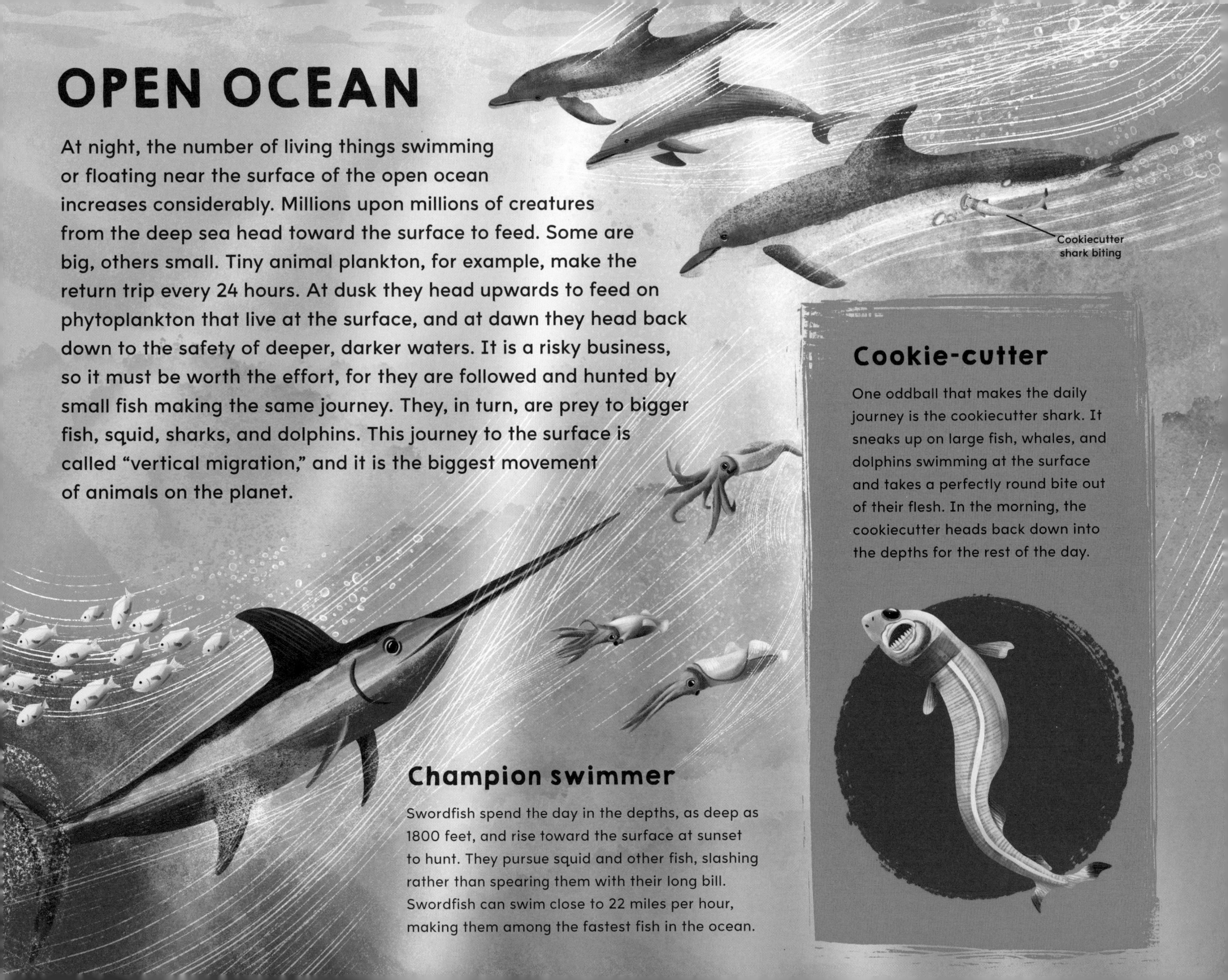

OPEN OCEAN

At night, the number of living things swimming or floating near the surface of the open ocean increases considerably. Millions upon millions of creatures from the deep sea head toward the surface to feed. Some are big, others small. Tiny animal plankton, for example, make the return trip every 24 hours. At dusk they head upwards to feed on phytoplankton that live at the surface, and at dawn they head back down to the safety of deeper, darker waters. It is a risky business, so it must be worth the effort, for they are followed and hunted by small fish making the same journey. They, in turn, are prey to bigger fish, squid, sharks, and dolphins. This journey to the surface is called "vertical migration," and it is the biggest movement of animals on the planet.

Cookiecutter shark biting

Cookie-cutter

One oddball that makes the daily journey is the cookiecutter shark. It sneaks up on large fish, whales, and dolphins swimming at the surface and takes a perfectly round bite out of their flesh. In the morning, the cookiecutter heads back down into the depths for the rest of the day.

Champion swimmer

Swordfish spend the day in the depths, as deep as 1800 feet, and rise toward the surface at sunset to hunt. They pursue squid and other fish, slashing rather than spearing them with their long bill. Swordfish can swim close to 22 miles per hour, making them among the fastest fish in the ocean.

Blubber-lips

Another unusual deep-sea shark is the megamouth. It is so rarely seen that it was only discovered in 1976, and fewer than 100 have been recorded since, so not much is known about it. One thing scientists do know is that the shark embarks on a daily vertical migration. It remains at a depth of 500 feet during the day and rises to 65 feet at night. It moves incredibly slowly—little more than 1 miles per hour. As its name suggests, the megamouth has a large mouth with rubbery lips, and it swims with the mouth wide open, sifting the water for tiny zooplankton, such as krill and jellyfish.

Jumbo squid

Humboldt, or jumbo, squid are big. They grow up to 8 feet long and have eight arms and two extendable tentacles. The tips of the tentacles have a club of suckers with sharp hooks, which the squid use to seize their prey. They spend the day in a part of the deep sea with low oxygen levels, so few other predators move into the same zone, making it a safe place to rest. At night, large groups of squid rise toward the surface to hunt. Shoals may include more than a thousand individuals, and the squid "talk" to each other with rapidly changing skin colors, flashing red and white. They eat all sorts of fish, and even other jumbo squid, since they are cannibals.

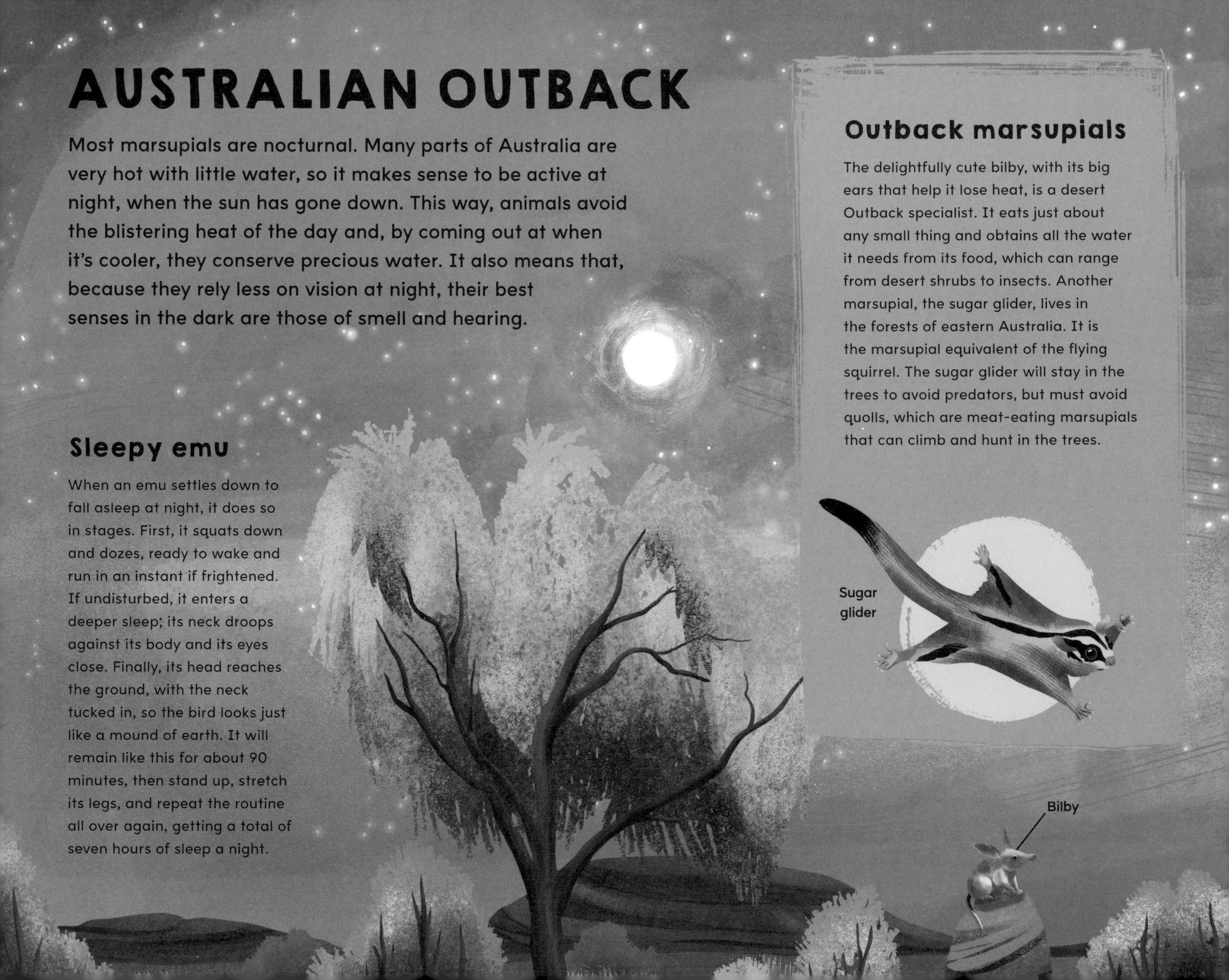

AUSTRALIAN OUTBACK

Most marsupials are nocturnal. Many parts of Australia are very hot with little water, so it makes sense to be active at night, when the sun has gone down. This way, animals avoid the blistering heat of the day and, by coming out at when it's cooler, they conserve precious water. It also means that, because they rely less on vision at night, their best senses in the dark are those of smell and hearing.

Sleepy emu

When an emu settles down to fall asleep at night, it does so in stages. First, it squats down and dozes, ready to wake and run in an instant if frightened. If undisturbed, it enters a deeper sleep; its neck droops against its body and its eyes close. Finally, its head reaches the ground, with the neck tucked in, so the bird looks just like a mound of earth. It will remain like this for about 90 minutes, then stand up, stretch its legs, and repeat the routine all over again, getting a total of seven hours of sleep a night.

Outback marsupials

The delightfully cute bilby, with its big ears that help it lose heat, is a desert Outback specialist. It eats just about any small thing and obtains all the water it needs from its food, which can range from desert shrubs to insects. Another marsupial, the sugar glider, lives in the forests of eastern Australia. It is the marsupial equivalent of the flying squirrel. The sugar glider will stay in the trees to avoid predators, but must avoid quolls, which are meat-eating marsupials that can climb and hunt in the trees.

Sugar glider

Bilby

Facing forward

The red kangaroo is the world's largest
living marsupial. Like most marsupials,
the female red kangaroo keeps its
underdeveloped baby, known as
a joey, in a pouch on its tummy.
In the kangaroo's case, the
entrance of the pouch
faces forward, but some
marsupials, such as the
wombat, have a pouch
with the entrance
facing backward.
This is because some
marsupials regularly
dig, and don't want
soil filling the pouch.

Square poo

The wombat is vulnerable to attacks by a type of
wild dog called the dingo. Its defense is to make
for the nearest burrow and block the entrance
with its backside, which is strengthened with extra
cartilage. Its claim to fame, though, is something
else entirely: its poo is in the shape of a cube!

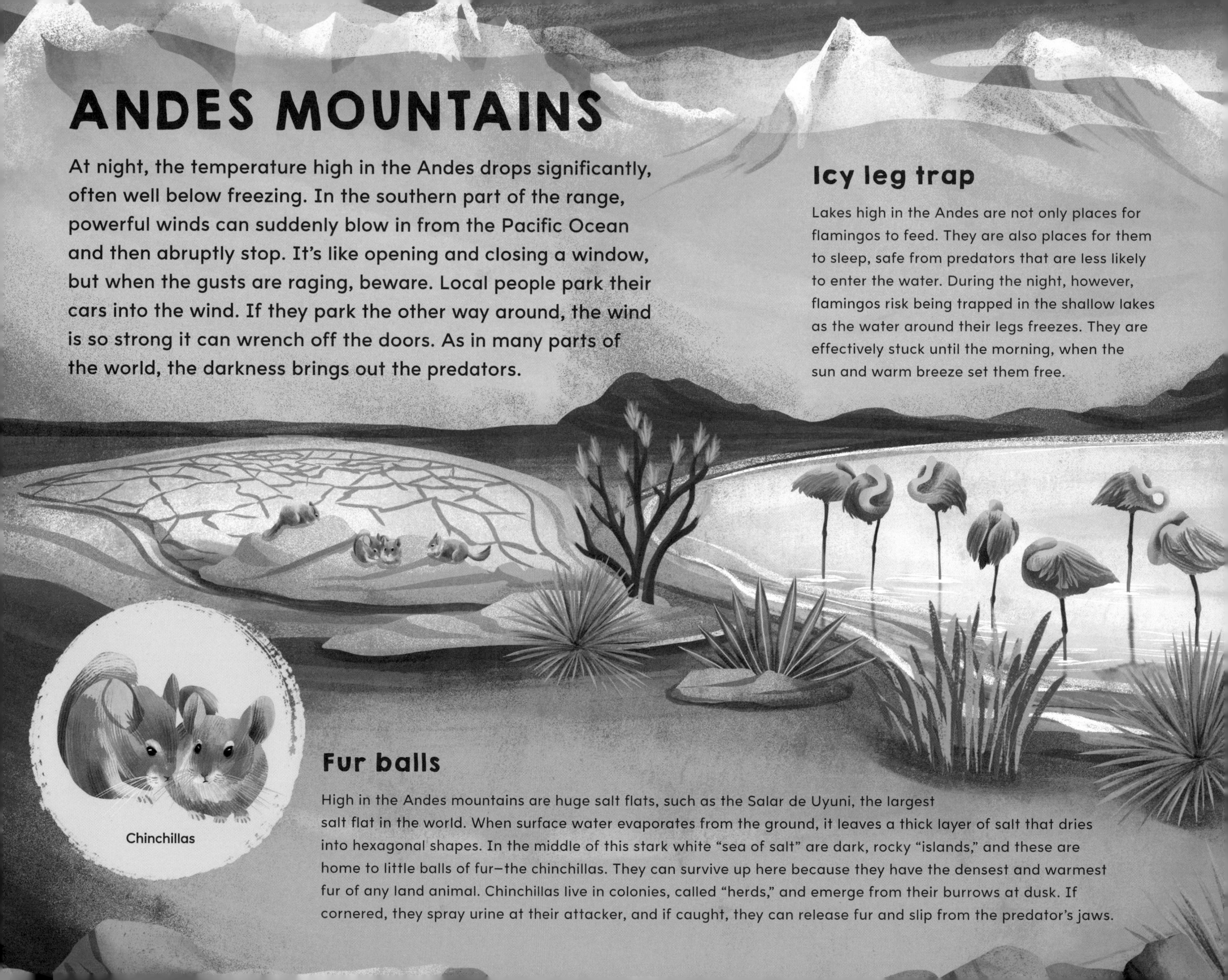

ANDES MOUNTAINS

At night, the temperature high in the Andes drops significantly, often well below freezing. In the southern part of the range, powerful winds can suddenly blow in from the Pacific Ocean and then abruptly stop. It's like opening and closing a window, but when the gusts are raging, beware. Local people park their cars into the wind. If they park the other way around, the wind is so strong it can wrench off the doors. As in many parts of the world, the darkness brings out the predators.

Icy leg trap

Lakes high in the Andes are not only places for flamingos to feed. They are also places for them to sleep, safe from predators that are less likely to enter the water. During the night, however, flamingos risk being trapped in the shallow lakes as the water around their legs freezes. They are effectively stuck until the morning, when the sun and warm breeze set them free.

Chinchillas

Fur balls

High in the Andes mountains are huge salt flats, such as the Salar de Uyuni, the largest salt flat in the world. When surface water evaporates from the ground, it leaves a thick layer of salt that dries into hexagonal shapes. In the middle of this stark white "sea of salt" are dark, rocky "islands," and these are home to little balls of fur—the chinchillas. They can survive up here because they have the densest and warmest fur of any land animal. Chinchillas live in colonies, called "herds," and emerge from their burrows at dusk. If cornered, they spray urine at their attacker, and if caught, they can release fur and slip from the predator's jaws.

Terror in the dark

Predators high in the Andes include the culpeo fox and the Andes mountain cat. They both hunt on the upper slopes of the mountains. The culpeo fox, also known as the zorro, mainly catches rodents, such as viscachas and degus, but will not turn down a vicuña carcass if it comes across a puma's kill. The ash-gray colored mountain cat is an expert at catching viscachas, which represent about 90 percent of its diet, and appears to be most successful on moonless nights, when the rodents are less likely to see the cat approaching.

Andes mountain cat

Viscachas

Degus

Culpeo fox

A cat by many names

The most formidable predator in the Andes is the puma, an animal that can be found from Alaska in North America to Tierra del Fuego at the tip of South America. In each country in which it resides, the puma has several different names, for example, in the United States alone it is known as a cougar, mountain lion, catamount, or panther. It is smaller than the guanaco, its main prey in the Andes, but that doesn't stop it. The puma is an ambush hunter. It uses the cover of darkness and the rough terrain to creep up on its unwary prey, which, despite the difference in size, it wrestles to the ground. At one time, scientists thought that pumas were solitary animals, but recent observations reveal that they sometimes meet at night and share their food with other pumas.

TROPICAL CORAL REEF

The coral city becomes a battleground at night. While parrotfish sleep in mucus sleeping bags and surgeonfish lock themselves into crevices using stiff fin spines, many types of sharks and other fish are out hunting. Sharks are remarkably efficient night hunters because they use a range of different senses, as well as vision, to locate their target. With an acute sense of smell, the shark can detect any odors associated with prey, for example, bodily fluids in the water. They can hear low-frequency sounds, such as a wounded fish thrashing around. Sensors in the shark's snout pick up the electrical fields generated by the prey's muscles, so the shark can home in precisely on the target, even with its eyes closed. Then, there are touch and taste. Typically the shark will take a test bite to see if potential food tastes good. It even has "touch at a distance," thanks to the lateral line of sensors that runs along the side of its body and picks up pressure changes in the water.

Reef edge patrols

At the edge of the reef, where it drops off into deep water, schools of gray reef sharks patrol. They search for fish along the edges of the coral wall and in the channels that connect shallow lagoons with the open sea. In the dark, giant manta rays swoop in from the ocean and scoop up swarms of animal plankton containing the young of crabs, lobsters, and fish, and tiger sharks move into the reef's central lagoon searching for the weak and the unwary. By morning, they are all gone, and the reef is relatively peaceful once more.

Moray
eel

Spears and hammers

Mantis shrimp are colorful predators that live in burrows and emerge at night to hunt. They possess weapons that would impress even the toughest video game characters. There are two types of mantis shrimp: spearers and smashers. The spearers tend to spear fish, while the smashers crack the shells of crabs and mollusks with a hammer. The weapons, which are modified claws, are unbelievably powerful and move at an incredible speed. Mantis shrimp kept in tanks have been known to break the glass.

spears

Mantis shrimp

smashers

Double jaws

Moray eels emerge from their daytime resting places among the corals and grab any fish, cuttlefish, or squid that pass by. The eel has two sets of jaws: one at the front of the mouth and the other at the back. The front jaws grab the prey and the second set pulls it into the throat. The shape of the jaws and teeth depends on the eel's main food. Species with round jaws and flat teeth feed on crabs, lobsters, and shrimp, while other eels have pointed jaws and sharp teeth that are good for catching fish.

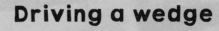

Driving a wedge

At dusk, whitetip reef sharks suddenly come to life. They leave their daytime resting places and, using their wedge-shaped heads, smash their way into cracks and crevices as they try to catch orange squirrelfish and soldierfish that are also active at night.

CITIES

Nighttime in the city is when all the pests come out—cockroaches, silverfish, house mice, brown and black rats, and slugs and snails. It's also when many invaders from the countryside feel it is safe to come out.

Cockroach

Silverfish

Scuttling pests

Cockroaches like warm, damp places where there is plenty of food, such as restaurant kitchens, fast-food restaurants and bakeries. Silverfish move into bathrooms, kitchens, and basements, where they feed on wallpaper adhesives, glue, book bindings, hair, and a host of other products found in the home.

New bodies and behavior

Some city invaders are remarkably different from their country cousins. In the United States, cotton mice and meadow voles that live in the city have bigger brains to cope with the complexities of urban life. Gray squirrels have given up on calling, because of the background noise, and instead communicate with each other through flicks of the tail. In the UK, city songbirds sing at a higher pitch to overcome the low-pitched rumble of traffic. All in all, it's remarkable that wildlife is changing our cities and our cities are changing wildlife.

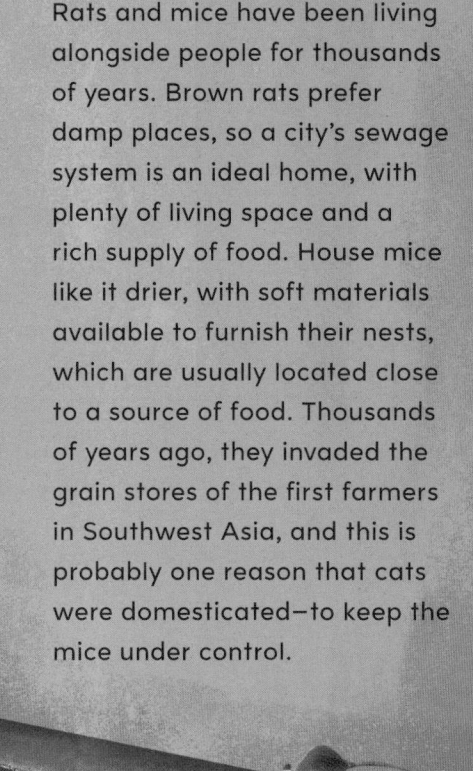

The faint sounds of mice scuttling about are focused on the tawny owl's ears by the feathers on its face.

Pesky rodents

Rats and mice have been living alongside people for thousands of years. Brown rats prefer damp places, so a city's sewage system is an ideal home, with plenty of living space and a rich supply of food. House mice like it drier, with soft materials available to furnish their nests, which are usually located close to a source of food. Thousands of years ago, they invaded the grain stores of the first farmers in Southwest Asia, and this is probably one reason that cats were domesticated—to keep the mice under control.

Countryside in the city

Racoons and opossums visit U.S. streets and backyards, while in the UK, these spaces are the domain of the red fox and European badger. There are said to be more foxes in London than double-decker buses. Tawny owls have reached the suburbs, and each night call with their familiar "Tu-whit, Tu-who", as William Shakespeare described their distinctive hoots in *Love's Labour's Lost*. One big surprise is that peregrines—usually active during the day—have started to hunt at night, using artificial light to help them catch other sleepless birds.

Slimy critters

Slugs and snails like dark and humid conditions too. They glide across the ground on a single, slimy foot, and in the morning, you can see their dried slime trails across paths. Taking about an hour to cover a few feet, they power along toward many a gardener's favorite plants, and effectively demolish them. A row of seedlings can be reduced to a sorry string of bare stalks by sunrise.

Playtime

In Russia's far north and around Canada's Hudson Bay, polar bears have moved into towns, and in Eastern Europe, brown bears may be encountered in the street at night. In the United States, brown and black bears have been seen diving into peoples' swimming pools and foxes have been recorded on security cameras jumping on children's trampolines. Beware, though, it's not all fun and games. In an Indian city, you may well come face to face with an angry leopard. Then it's time to lock yourself indoors, and don't even risk taking a look!

Desert rabbit

Animals living in hot deserts are often crepuscular, so they avoid the heat of the day and the chill of the night. The desert cottontail of North America hides for most of the day in brushy scrub, and its large ears help keep its body cool by losing heat like a radiator, similar to the ears of the fennec fox. It is mainly active at dawn and dusk and gets its name from the white patch of fur on its tail that resembles a cotton ball. The rabbit raises its tail when danger is near to warn other cottontails, and the whiteness is clearly visible in twilight. If it has to escape, it can run at 20 miles per hour in a zigzag pattern to fool its pursuers.

Hunting dogs

In the Australian Outback, wildlife must be wary at dusk, because that's when the dingo comes out to hunt. It is a dog from Southeast Asia that was probably brought to Australia by its first people. Today, though, it is a wild animal rather than a domestic one. It hunts, emus, kangaroos, wallabies and any other animals it might come across, including the livestock on farms, so some people consider it a pest.

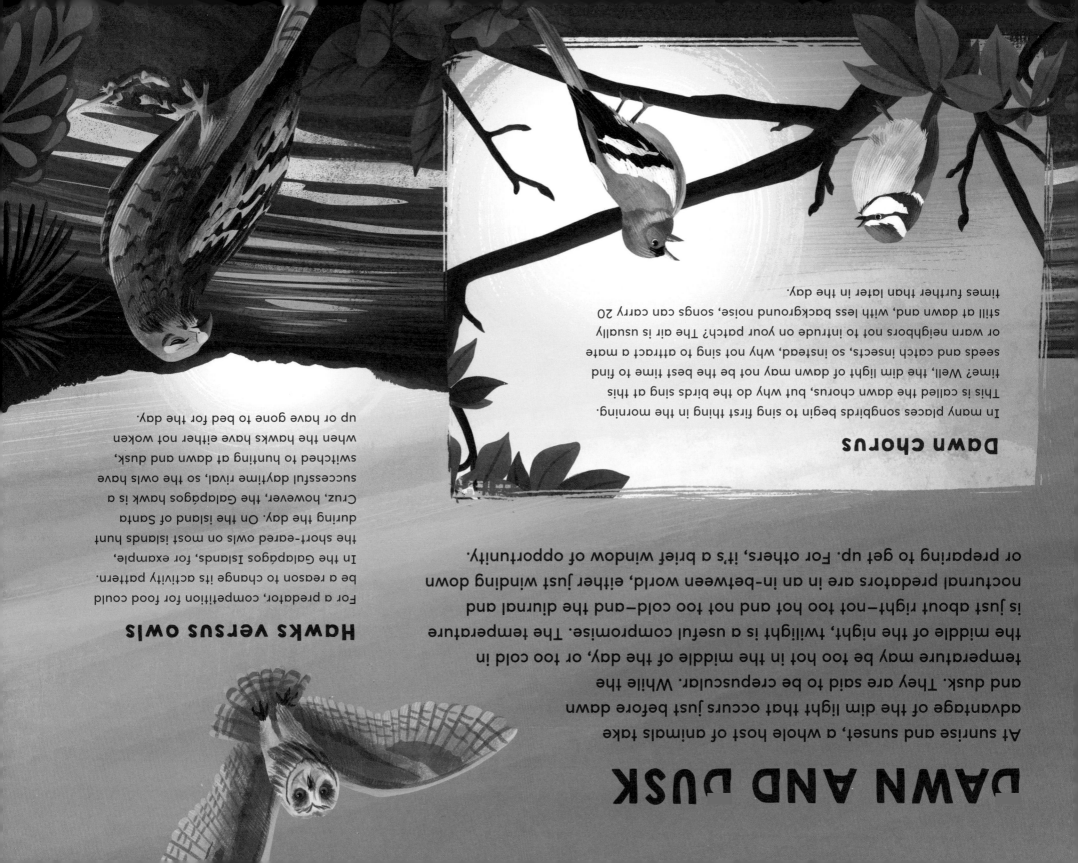

DAWN AND DUSK

At sunrise and sunset, a whole host of animals take advantage of the dim light that occurs just before dawn and dusk. They are said to be crepuscular. While the temperature may be too hot in the middle of the day, or too cold in the middle of the night, twilight is a useful compromise. The temperature is just about right—not too hot and not too cold—and the diurnal and nocturnal predators are in an in-between world, either just winding down or preparing to get up. For others, it's a brief window of opportunity.

Hawks versus owls

For a predator, competition for food could be a reason to change its activity pattern. In the Galápagos Islands, for example, the short-eared owls on most islands hunt during the day. On the island of Santa Cruz, however, the Galápagos hawk is a successful daytime rival, so the owls have switched to hunting at dawn and dusk, when the hawks have either not woken up or have gone to bed for the day.

Dawn chorus

In many places songbirds begin to sing first thing in the morning. This is called the dawn chorus, but why do the birds sing at this time? Well, the dim light of dawn may not be the best time to find seeds and catch insects, so instead, why not sing to attract a mate or warn neighbors not to intrude on your patch? The air is usually still at dawn and, with less background noise, songs can carry 20 times further than later in the day.

words&pictures

CONTENTS

DAYTIME ANIMALS

Animals that are active during the daytime are said to be diurnal. They hunt or forage by day and sleep, rest, or hide during the hours of darkness. Most monkeys and all of the apes, including humans, are diurnal animals. So, too, are many birds and the majority of animals that rely on the sun to warm up each morning to become active, such as many types of snakes and lizards.

See and not be seen

Many daytime animals—both predators and prey— rely on good eyesight to survive. During the day, the sense of vision is just as important for animals that have to be alert to danger approaching as it is for the animals that try to catch them.

Wraparound vision

Plant eaters (herbivores), such as antelope and gazelles, have their eyes on the sides of their heads, so they can spot danger approaching from almost any direction, but they cannot see predators approaching from directly behind them. Many have good hearing and a good sense of smell to help provide an early warning, but vision is vital for them to see an attacker and take evasive action.

Facing forward

Many predators, such as birds of prey and big cats, have eyes on the front of their head, giving them binocular vision like most humans have. With this, they can calculate the distance to their prey and whether it is moving toward or away from them. The champions are eagles, which can spot their prey on the ground from miles away, even when they are high in the sky. These predators are all active during the day because that's when the animals they try to catch are active too.

Daytime eyes

At the back of our eyes is a layer of light-sensitive cells (the retina). There are two main types of cells: rods and cones. Rods are highly sensitive to light and cones are for color. We humans have both, so we can see clearly and in color. Other diurnal animals with eyes like ours have the same cells, and most also have relatively small eyes with round pupils like we do.

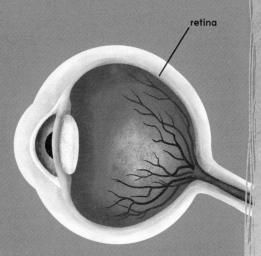

retina

Human eye

Attractive colors

Flowers that open in daytime and display colorful petals want to attract day-flying insects, such as honeybees and butterflies, to help pollinate them. The insects use their eyes, more than any of their other senses, to find the flowers.

Day-night switching

Some animals that are normally active at night can switch to coming out in the day. Rats, for example, are primarily nocturnal animals, but if their home area is invaded by night-hunting foxes, the rats become diurnal, to avoid getting caught.

SOUTH AMERICAN RAIN FOREST

The Amazon rain forest lies within the Tropics. Here the morning may start with bright sunshine but, by afternoon, thunderstorms often roll in and torrential rain falls. This happens for about 200 days of the year—and it's the reason we call it a rain forest. The Amazon basin spreads out on either side of the Equator, where the amount of daylight is roughly the same all year round. How much sunlight an animal receives, though, depends on the level at which it lives in the forest. Those in the branches of the canopy see the most, while those on the forest floor experience the least. This is because the trees are packed so tightly together that their leaves block out the sun from the lower levels.

Red-faced monkey

One of the strangest-looking monkeys in the canopy is the bald uakari. Early explorers thought its bright crimson face resembled that of a bald-headed and sunburned Englishman, and they poked fun at it, but in the case of the bald uakari, the redder the face, the healthier the animal. It feeds mainly on seeds, and the teeth in its powerful lower jaw are shaped in such a way that it can open unripe fruits to get at the seeds inside. This gives the uakari an advantage over other Amazon monkeys, because they have to wait until the fruits ripen.

Treetop killer

One of the main predators in the treetops is the harpy eagle. It's one of the world's largest birds of prey and has the most powerful talons of any living eagle. It perches in a tree until it spots a target, and then swoops in and grabs it. The harpy eagle is so strong that it can pluck a monkey or sloth from a branch and fly away without having to land.

Blue morpho butterfly

Clay licks

Where the river has eroded the riverbank, the exposed wall of clay attracts colorful and boisterous macaws. These birds arrive each morning to eat the clay. Scientists are not sure why they do this, but it is probably either to take in certain minerals, such as sodium, that are absent from their normal diet or to neutralize poisons that are present in the unripe fruits and seeds that they eat.

Monster rodent

The world's largest rodent gathers in groups on riverbanks and islands. It is called the capybara, and it looks like a giant guinea pig. It spends some of its day in the water, feeding on aquatic plants, and emerges to chomp on grasses in summer and reeds in winter. The capybara's lower jaw is hinged in such a way that it chews food back and forth, rather than side to side like other plant eaters.

AFRICAN SAVANNA

The gently undulating grasslands of the African savanna have only a scattering of trees in which to hide, so many of the animals living here rely on speed to hunt prey or stay out of trouble. They include some of the speediest land animals on Earth, like the cheetah (the fastest animal on four legs) and the ostrich (the quickest bird on two legs). With the sun beating down relentlessly and little shade, many animals rest in the middle of the day—all except the cheetah. As a relatively small cat, it hunts when the larger predators, such as lions and leopards, are taking a break, so it does not have to fight or compete with them for food.

Following the rains

On the savanna, there are dry seasons and rainy seasons. The grasslands are at their best during the rains, when they provide food for millions of plant eaters—the wildebeest, gazelles, and zebras. The wildebeest have the uncanny knack of knowing where rain is falling in the distance, and they lead the other herbivores in one of the greatest migrations on Earth...and wherever the plant eaters go, the meat eaters are never far behind.

Hunting alone

The cheetah is generally a solitary hunter. It has black "tears" below the eyes to help keep the sun's glare from reflecting off its fur, like the black under-eye paint used by football and baseball players. The cheetah is also a champion sprinter, accelerating to 60 miles per hour in a few seconds, although most of its hunts are slower. It uses its speed to catch fleet-footed gazelles. Female cheetahs tend to hunt alone, but to bring down anything bigger, such as an ostrich or topi, several male cheetahs sometimes work together, like lions.

Hunting together

Lions hunt in small groups known as prides. Each pride has a handful of adult females and their cubs, and they are all protected by two or more males. The females mainly do the hunting, although males sometimes join in. By working together, the lions can hunt prey far bigger than themselves, such as buffalo and zebras, although they usually opt for a wildebeest, because there are so many of them. Some large prides have been known to tackle elephants.

Feisty monkeys

Olive baboons forage for roots and tubers on the savanna floor, but if they are surprised by a leopard, they make for the trees. The leopard is an accomplished climber, but fortunately for the baboons, it is too heavy to reach the topmost branches. If the leopard catches a baboon on the ground, the rest of the troop do something unexpected. Instead of running away, they run toward the big cat, mobbing it until the leopard lets go.

10

NORTH AMERICAN PRAIRIES

In the middle of the North American continent are vast areas of grassland known as prairies. The main vegetation is grass, with wildflowers and few trees. Temperatures are generally mild, rainfall is moderate, and the soils are fertile, so much of the prairies has been turned into farmland for growing wheat. There are still wild areas remaining, and others have been returned to their natural state, so wildlife still has a place to live.

Bald eagle

Living battering ram

North America's largest living animal is the bison, also called the buffalo. Great herds once roamed the prairies, but now there are far fewer. They are important to the prairies because their sharp hooves churn up the ground like a plow, preventing the soil from becoming waterlogged, and their constant grazing keeps the grasses healthy. For most of the year they are gentle, although unpredictable, and they are most active at breeding time, when bulls engage in ferocious head-banging fights to become top bison.

Long-distance runner

The prairies are home to another speedster—the pronghorn. Resembling an antelope, the pronghorn can reach a top speed of 55 miles per hour and run fast for long periods. It's a long-distance runner rather than a sprinter. Why the pronghorn needed to run so fast for so long was a mystery, because most North American predators, such as wolves and bears, cannot match its speed. Then a scientist discovered that, not too long ago, there were cheetahs in North America, and the pronghorn needed speed to escape from them. Today, the cheetahs are extinct...but the pronghorn still keeps running.

Greater prairie chicken

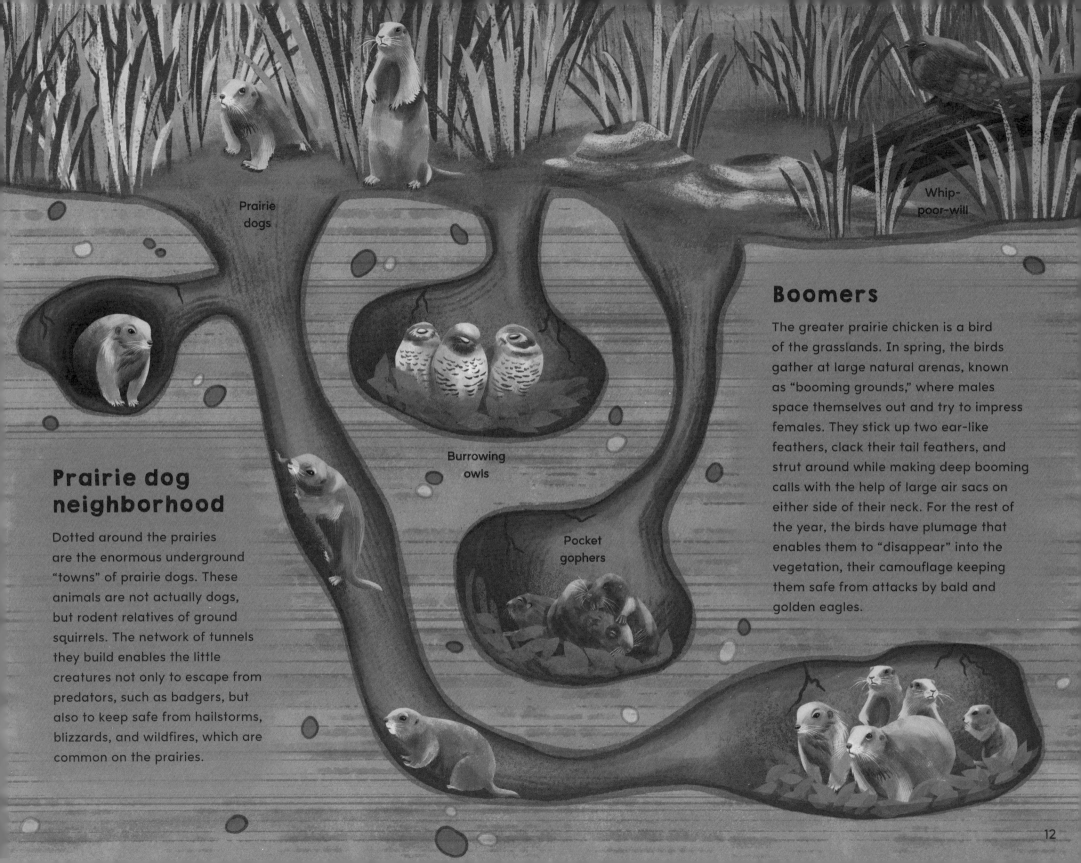

Prairie dogs

Whip-poor-will

Boomers

The greater prairie chicken is a bird of the grasslands. In spring, the birds gather at large natural arenas, known as "booming grounds," where males space themselves out and try to impress females. They stick up two ear-like feathers, clack their tail feathers, and strut around while making deep booming calls with the help of large air sacs on either side of their neck. For the rest of the year, the birds have plumage that enables them to "disappear" into the vegetation, their camouflage keeping them safe from attacks by bald and golden eagles.

Burrowing owls

Pocket gophers

Prairie dog neighborhood

Dotted around the prairies are the enormous underground "towns" of prairie dogs. These animals are not actually dogs, but rodent relatives of ground squirrels. The network of tunnels they build enables the little creatures not only to escape from predators, such as badgers, but also to keep safe from hailstorms, blizzards, and wildfires, which are common on the prairies.

EUROPEAN WOODLAND

European woodlands have trees that lose their leaves in winter, such as oak, ash, beech, and horse chestnut—all trees with broad, rather than needlelike, leaves. The reason is not the cold, but drought. In winter the water in the soil is often frozen, so it is not available to the trees. It is like being in a desert—an icy cold one. Trees lose water through their leaves in a process called transpiration, so, by discarding their leaves in winter, the trees reduce their water loss and survive the harshest time of the year.

Busy forest canopy

In the trees, woodpeckers hammer the trunks to announce they are in residence, jays collect acorns, song thrushes smash snail shells, and smaller songbirds collect seeds and caterpillars—but they must all watch out. They can easily be surprised by the sparrowhawk, which can maneuver among the branches and pin down a victim.

Beaver dam

Aerial dogfights

One of the most stunning butterflies in European woods is the purple emperor. Though beautiful, the males are very aggressive. They fly around the canopy of their "master" tree and, like warplanes, they chase away any other males and even other types of butterfly that venture onto their patch. They welcome female purple emperors, but if one has already mated, she drops out of the air like a stone to get away.

Beware of bears

While there are many wild boar and thousands of deer (including roe deer, fallow deer, and moose) in Europe's woodlands, they keep out of sight and are so well camouflaged that we rarely see them. A brown bear, though, will smell them, since it has one of the most sensitive noses in the animal world.

Charming but cunning

Stoats are brave little critters. They hunt animals five times their size, such as rabbits. They are just as good at climbing trees (where they steal birds' eggs) as they are at running through the underground burrows of wood mice and voles. They are active mainly during the day in spring, but hunt day and night in fall. The black tip of their tail is thought to distract birds of prey, so the birds try to grab the tail rather than the stoat's body.

SAHARA DESERT

The Sahara is the world's largest hot desert. It sits in the northern half of Africa and covers an area a little bigger than the United States. It's a harsh place for plants and animals to live. Fierce winds scour the sands and rocks, and the temperature during the day averages 86°F all year round—and can rise to 136°F, one of the highest recorded air temperatures on Earth. There is almost no rain in some parts of the desert, and little water on the surface, but deep beneath it are huge reservoirs of ground water that seep out in some places to form oases. These pockets of water and vegetation are magnets for desert wildlife and fueling stops for birds on their migration across the Sahara.

Desert antelope

The hot desert is not a comfortable place to be during the middle of the day, but there is life here. The addax is a large, endangered antelope that has ways to survive the heat and dryness. It is active during the cooler parts of the day, and when it gets too hot, small groups of addax lie together in shady depressions. The addax gets all the water it needs from the plants it eats and from dew that forms on foliage at night. It also has special pockets in its stomach that store water for when times get tough.

Addax

Share with a friend

A number of birds call the Sahara home. One of these is the greater hoopoe lark, a small songbird with a long, curved beak and tall, spindly legs. It seems to run more than it flies, chasing insects on the ground. Like the cheetah, the lark has black lines across and below the eyes that may help absorb sunlight and reduce the amount of glare entering its eyes. It has also evolved a clever behavior to cope in the heat. When the temperature soars and the surface of the sand can reach 144°F, the lark heads for the shelter of a spiny-tailed lizard's burrow. The lizard is a vegetarian, so the lark is safe, and being underground reduces the bird's water loss by as much as 80 percent.

While the cat's away

Most of the desert animals active in the daytime are small. The sandfish, for example, is a slender lizard that moves over and under the sand at high speed, so it looks as if it swims. In the middle of the day, it hides from the sun under the sand. This is the cue for silver ants to make their move. With their number one predator resting, they forage while the desert is at its hottest, darting out of their underground nest and back, using the sun to navigate and ensure they don't get lost. A fine silver "fur" helps protect them from the sun's rays, but if they stay too long in the open, they will be, quite literally, "toast."

16

SOUTHEAST ASIA CAVES AND FORESTS

The gaping mouth of a huge cave on the island of Borneo is like a busy intersection. It is a place where millions of wrinkle-lipped bats and cave swiftlets pass one another when traveling between sleeping and nesting sites inside the cave and hunting sites in the surrounding forests. It's also where predators take full advantage of the confusion at dawn and dusk, as the animals of the day shift and night shift switch places.

Bird exit

Cave swiftlets build their cup-shaped nests out of dried spit. They also use their saliva to glue their nests high on the side of the cave's vertical walls. Up there, they and their chicks are safe from predators, such as cave crickets and giant centipedes, which live on the floor and ledges of the cave. Each morning, millions of them must leave their nests and fly out into the forest. While in flight, they catch insects in mid-air.

Self-imposed imprisonment

The surrounding rain forest is rich in wildlife. Up in the trees lives the rhinoceros hornbill. It has a huge bill with a brightly colored helmet-like structure on top, known as a casque. At nesting time, the female enters a tree hollow and the male blocks up the entrance with mud, which dries and hardens, so she and her chicks are safe from tree snakes. The male must deliver her all her food through a small hole until the chicks are ready to fly. Only then will the birds chip away the dried mud and escape their nesting "prison."

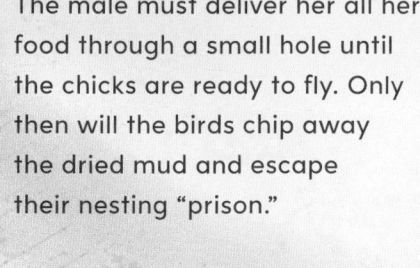

Exit dangers

On their way out, the cave swiftlets must run the gauntlet of cave racer snakes that hang down from stalactites inside the cave and grab birds as they fly by. Outside the cave entrance are bat hawks, which swoop down and seize birds from the departing flock.

Keeping dry

Monkeys and apes, such as grizzled langurs and orangutans, forage in the trees. The langur lives in small groups and eats leaves and shoots, and sometimes unripe fruits. The orangutan generally forages alone, which is unusual for an ape, and has been known to eat 400 different foods. When it rains, it covers its head with large leaves, just like an umbrella.

Giant cave centipede

Long-legged giant centipedes don't have 100 legs, but just 15 pairs. Unusually for centipedes, they hunt by day. They kill insects and worms by injecting venom from sharp "fangs."

Pigs with a beard

On the forest floor, bearded pigs and muntjac deer feed on flowers, fruits, and leaves. At one time, the pigs and deer had to watch out for tigers, but not any more —the tigers on the island of Borneo are thought to be extinct.

AN ISLAND APART: MADAGASCAR

Off the coast of southeast Africa, the island of Madagascar and almost all of its wildlife separated from the mainland millions of years ago. This means that many of the animals that live there are found nowhere else on Earth. While monkeys and apes, for example, spread across Africa, they are absent from Madagascar. They never made it to the island, but another group of primates did—the lemurs. Lemurs probably drifted on rafts across the narrow strip of sea, and now they are found in all the places in Madagascar where monkeys would be expected to live.

Island of chameleons

Madagascar is home to half of the world's many different types of chameleons, and one of the largest is the panther chameleon, at 20 inches long. It has an exceptionally long tongue, which, when stretched out, can be double the length of the chameleon's body. The tongue shoots out of the chameleon's mouth at five times the acceleration reached by a jet fighter, so few insects within range get away. The chameleon can also change color, becoming darker when it wants to warm up in the morning or when confronting a rival. It doesn't, however, change color to match its surroundings.

Apex predator

The cat-like fossa looks like a small puma, but it is not a cat. It has paws and claws like a cat, a tail like a monkey, and round ears like a weasel, but is more closely related to the mongoose. The fossa, which is active day and night, is the top predator on the island—and a lemur's worst enemy.

Dancing lemur

The tree-dwelling sifaka sometimes comes down to the ground in order to move from one tree to the next. When it does so, it crosses the ground on its back legs only. It resembles a ballet dancer progressing elegantly across the forest floor.

Stink fights

Ring-tailed lemurs are daytime animals. They live in groups that are very territorial, and sometimes have "stink fights" with neighbors. They rub a fruity-smelling scent from special glands on their wrists and chest onto their black-and-white striped tails and wave them at their opponents. The smelliest team wins!

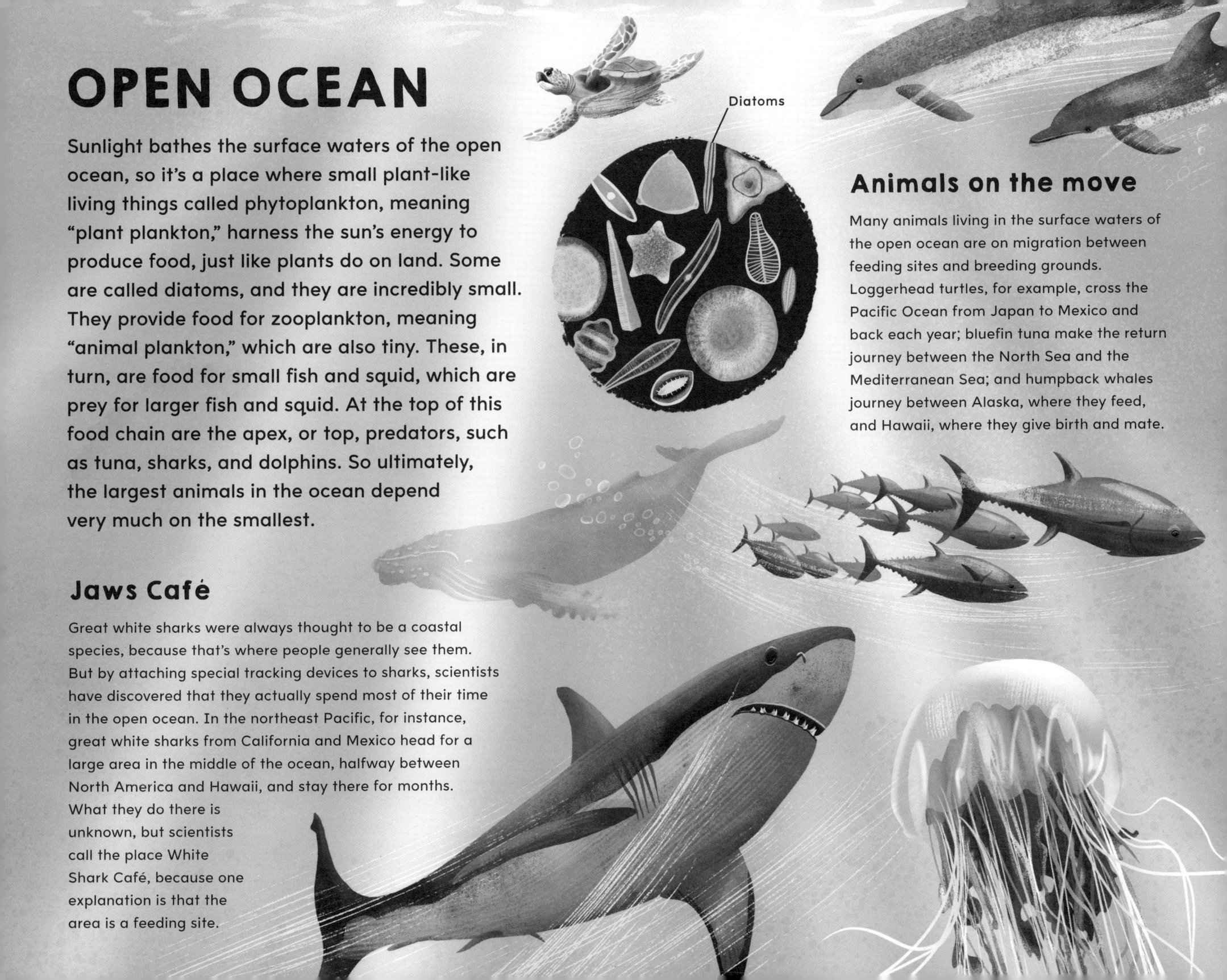

OPEN OCEAN

Sunlight bathes the surface waters of the open ocean, so it's a place where small plant-like living things called phytoplankton, meaning "plant plankton," harness the sun's energy to produce food, just like plants do on land. Some are called diatoms, and they are incredibly small. They provide food for zooplankton, meaning "animal plankton," which are also tiny. These, in turn, are food for small fish and squid, which are prey for larger fish and squid. At the top of this food chain are the apex, or top, predators, such as tuna, sharks, and dolphins. So ultimately, the largest animals in the ocean depend very much on the smallest.

Diatoms

Animals on the move

Many animals living in the surface waters of the open ocean are on migration between feeding sites and breeding grounds. Loggerhead turtles, for example, cross the Pacific Ocean from Japan to Mexico and back each year; bluefin tuna make the return journey between the North Sea and the Mediterranean Sea; and humpback whales journey between Alaska, where they feed, and Hawaii, where they give birth and mate.

Jaws Café

Great white sharks were always thought to be a coastal species, because that's where people generally see them. But by attaching special tracking devices to sharks, scientists have discovered that they actually spend most of their time in the open ocean. In the northeast Pacific, for instance, great white sharks from California and Mexico head for a large area in the middle of the ocean, halfway between North America and Hawaii, and stay there for months. What they do there is unknown, but scientists call the place White Shark Café, because one explanation is that the area is a feeding site.

Gigantic fish

Whale sharks are the world's biggest fish—the largest known was over 60 feet long. Where the sharks travel in the open ocean is mostly a mystery, but at certain times of the year these giants migrate to coastal waters. They arrive at the exact same time that fish are spawning, and the sharks gobble up their eggs. They sift the eggs from the water, so they are known as filter feeders. The fish, though, produce so many eggs that some escape the shark's mouth, which is 5 feet wide and shaped like a mailbox. Just a day later baby fish hatch and float around the ocean as part of the plankton.

Giant plankton

Jellyfish usually drift with the ocean currents, although they can also use their bodies to move. They open and close their bell-shaped bodies like somebody opening and closing an umbrella. One of the biggest is the lion's mane jellyfish, which can even survive in the cold waters of the Arctic Ocean. Its bell can be 6.6 feet across, and its stinging tentacles trail 98 feet below.

AUSTRALIAN OUTBACK

The Outback is not a single habitat, but a number of different wilderness areas—deserts, woodlands, savanna, lakes, mountains, and plains. These places, together with several nearby islands, are home to two groups of mammals that are unlike any others: the monotremes and marsupials. Monotremes have fur and feed their babies milk, like other mammals, but they lay eggs, like reptiles. Marsupials give birth to their young when they are very small and not well developed, so in many species (but not all), the babies are kept in a pouch on the mother's body until they are ready for the outside world.

Big bird

The emu is the world's second tallest bird, after the ostrich—it can be up to 6 feet tall. Emus are active during the day when they forage, preen, and dust bathe, and they tend to live in pairs. They are fast runners, reaching a top speed of about 30 miles per hour, and they flap their tiny wings to help steady their bodies and keep themselves from falling over. Their feet have sharp claws that can be used in defense, and they have a special extra eyelid that acts like goggles to keep out dust.

A trio of reptiles

Lizards living in the Outback include the ferocious perentie monitor lizard, one of the world's largest lizards; the bizarre frilled lizard, which, when faced with danger, erects a flap of skin around its neck; and the thorny devil, which lives in the desert and collects dew on its hard, protective spines in the early morning, letting the water dribble through grooves down to its mouth.

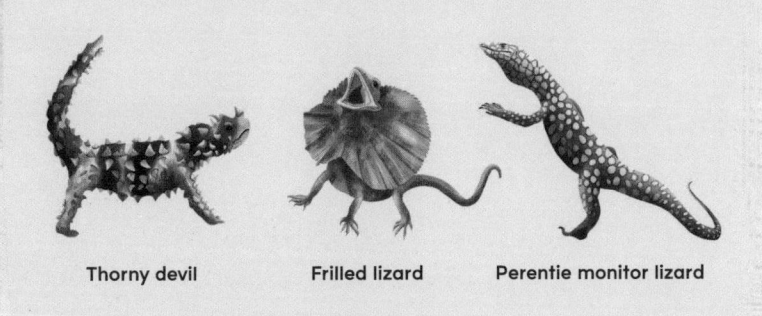

Thorny devil   Frilled lizard   Perentie monitor lizard

Wild parakeets

The familiar pet parakeet is a wild bird in Australia. It travels in small groups, but at times of drought can gather in huge flocks at water holes to drink. The seeds the parakeets eat have very little water in them, so they must find freshwater regularly. When they do, they must beware of birds of prey, such as goshawks and black kites, which are attracted to the noise of the parakeets' constant chattering.

termite mound

Termite specialist

The numbat is a rare and endangered marsupial living in the wild only in Western Australia. Unlike other marsupials, the female doesn't have a pouch. Her undeveloped young attach to her nipples to drink her milk, and they hang there for four or five months, protected only by folds of skin and fur. Later in life they ride on her back. The adults feed on termites, consuming up to 20,000 a day, but don't eat ants. They forage only during daylight hours, and retreat to burrows if it gets too hot or too cold.

Spiny anteater

The short-beaked echidna, or spiny anteater, is a monotreme. It is a hedgehog-like mammal, and it feeds on ants and termites. Its front feet have claws for breaking into ant and termite colonies, and its snout has special sensors that can detect the minute electrical fields produced by insects' muscles, so it can find them easily. This is a sense that is usually found in freshwater or marine animals, so the echidna may be the only land animal that can do this.

Deadly snake

Australia is full of highly venomous snakes, and many hunt in the day. The most venomous is the inland taipan. Although it is the most toxic snake on Earth, few people have been bitten, because it's quite shy. It is most active in the early morning. Most snakes bite and then let go, waiting for the prey to die, but the inland taipan strikes accurately several times, injecting venom deep into the prey, so it dies almost instantly. The snake's venom is designed to kill warm-blooded mammals, which includes us, and it's so powerful that the venom from a single bite could kill 100 adult humans.

ANDES MOUNTAINS

The Andes mountain range stretches the entire length of South America's western edge, from tropical Venezuela in the north to the colder parts of Chile in the south, making it the longest continental mountain range in the world.

Slow and fast walkers

Flamingos are birds you might associate with warm places, but high in the Andes three types of flamingos gather at salt lakes, where they feed on shrimp and algae. How fast they walk when feeding depends on their food. Those that feed on diatoms (algae) floating in the water walk at a stately 10–15 steps per minute, while those feeding on shrimp hurtle along at 40–60 steps per minute to stir up the bottom sediments and disturb the shrimp.

Shrimp

Living glider

The upper zones in the Andes Mountains are rich in wildlife, including one of the world's biggest flying birds. The Andean condor is a giant New World vulture with a 11 foot-wingspan. It uses those massive wings to soar on air currents that sweep up the sides of mountains or on rising bubbles of warm air, known as thermals, as it searches the slopes for the carcasses of dead animals. The condor is such a good glider that it flaps its wings on takeoff, but hardly at all when in the air.

Rabbit imposter

Between the snow line, where the uppermost zone of ice and snow starts, and the tree line, where the last of the forests grow, lies an area of loose rocks and moorland terrain. Here lives the viscacha, a furry rodent with big ears and long back legs. It looks like a rabbit with a long, bushy tail, but it isn't related to the rabbit at all. Its habitat has sparse vegetation, but by hiding out on steep rocky slopes, it can avoid being gobbled up by one of the many small predators up here, such as the Andean mountain cat and the culpeo fox. The viscacha forages for grasses and other mountain plants after dawn and from late afternoon to early evening. It spends the rest of the day sunbathing.

Plant-eating bears

Slightly lower down the mountain, there are cloud forests. They get their name from the way they are frequently enveloped in low cloud. The dampness encourages mosses to grow all over, on the ground and on trees. The trees themselves are generally shorter than in other forests, and they are decorated with bromeliads—flowering plants that grow on the bark of trees. Living here is an animal that's quite unexpected—the spectacled bear. It is the only species of bear in South America, and it climbs trees to feed on the bromeliads.

South American camels

Mountain pastures and rocky slopes are the domain of the guanaco, the wild relative of the llama. It lives in small herds, and male guanacos engage in violent fights for the right to occupy a prime site through which herds of female guanacos might pass. The opponents slam into each other and try to bite off one another's private parts. The guanaco is one of two wild relatives of the camel that live in the Andes, the other being the more delicate vicuña. Both are targeted by pumas.

TROPICAL CORAL REEF

Tropical coral reefs grow in warm, shallow seas. They are formed of tiny sea anemone-like animals known as coral polyps. In among the structures they build is a great diversity of colorful creatures, such as parrotfish, damselfish, butterflyfish, brightly colored shrimp, crabs, and lobsters. The reef is like a city, with high-rise coral "buildings" separated by avenues of sand and rock—and it is a city that never sleeps.

Sleepers and marauders

Some sharks hunt during the day, while others rest. Blacktip reef sharks dart around, chasing shoals of young fish in the sandy shallows, while whitetip reef sharks rest under overhanging rocks and in caves. Unlike many other types of sharks, which need to keep moving to breathe, the whitetip can actively pump water over its gills, so it can lie on the seabed.

Shark that walks on land

The top predators in and around the tropical coral reef are sharks and rays, and there is one little shark that can do the most extraordinary thing. At low tide, the epaulette shark is able to walk on its fins from one rock pool to another. This way, it can make sure it is always in the most comfortable place, one that's not too hot and which has sufficient oxygen for it to survive until the tide comes in again.

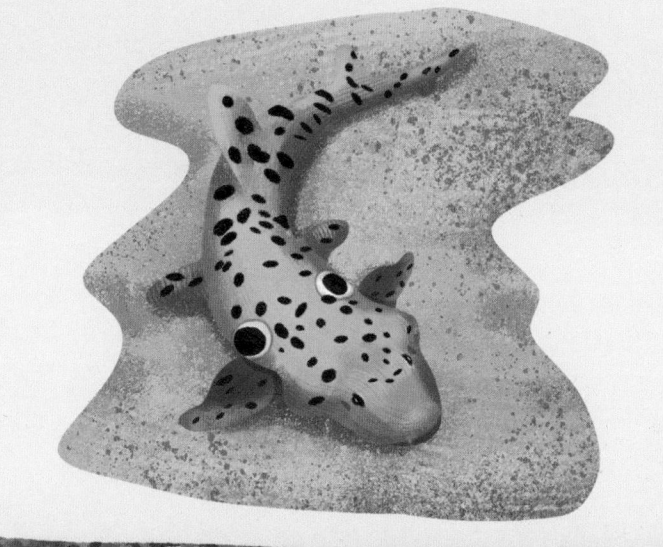

Bearded shark

During the day, the wobbegong, a type of carpet shark, uses camouflage to catch a meal. It lies on the floor of the coral reef, tucked under some coral, and waits for prey to come close. Its color blends in with the sandy background, and it has tassels around its mouth that look like seaweed. On its tail is a spot that, when it is waved around, looks like the eye of a small fish, and the wobbegong uses it to lure in a potential meal.

Wobbegong

Finding Nemo at home

The clownfish lives among the stinging tentacles of sea anemones. The two creatures help one another: the anemone defends the fish from its predators and the fish protects the anemone from parasites that grow on its surface. The brightly colored fish may also lure prey toward the anemone's venomous tentacles. The fish picks up scraps from the anemone's meal, and provides the anemone with food in the form of poo.

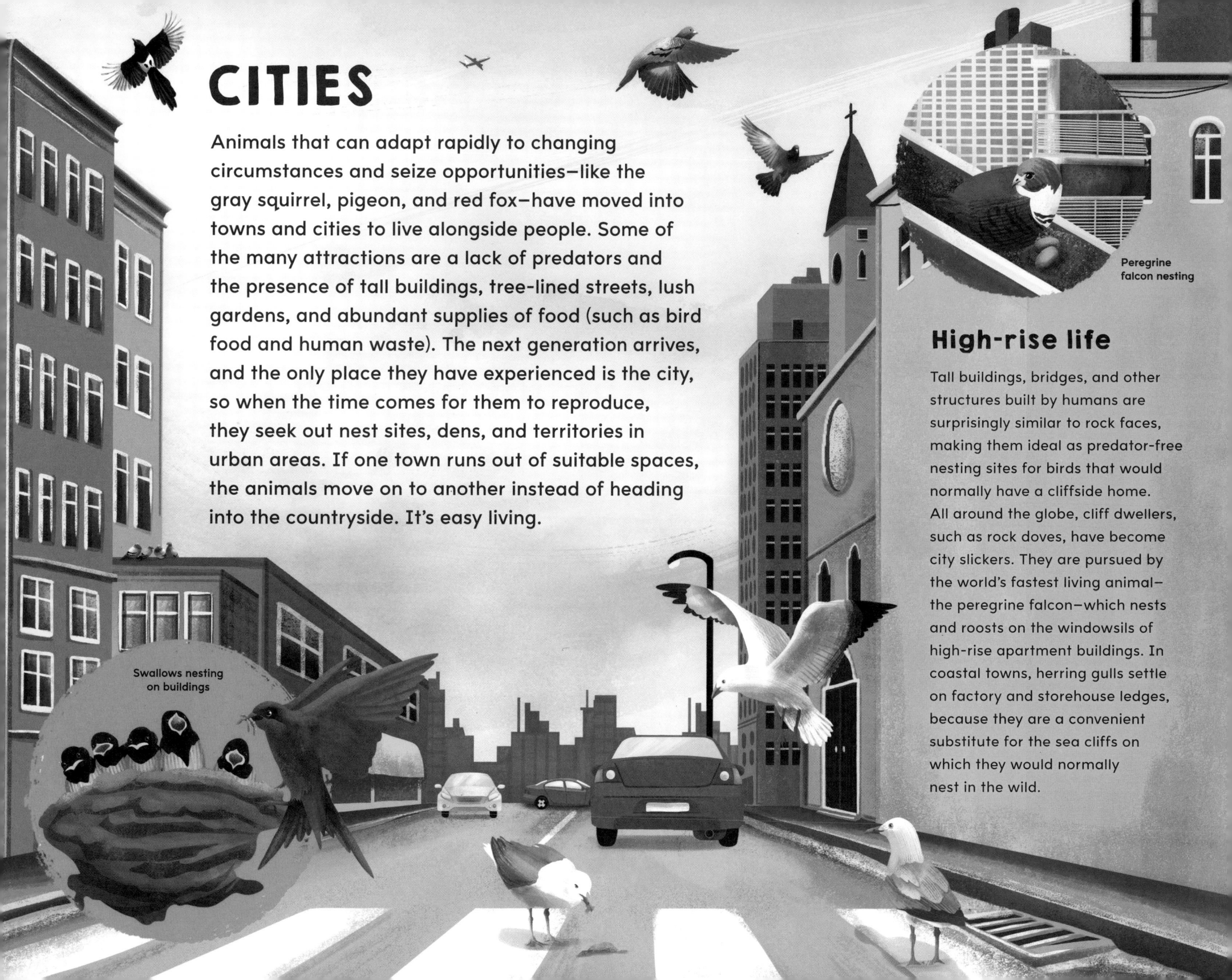

CITIES

Animals that can adapt rapidly to changing circumstances and seize opportunities—like the gray squirrel, pigeon, and red fox—have moved into towns and cities to live alongside people. Some of the many attractions are a lack of predators and the presence of tall buildings, tree-lined streets, lush gardens, and abundant supplies of food (such as bird food and human waste). The next generation arrives, and the only place they have experienced is the city, so when the time comes for them to reproduce, they seek out nest sites, dens, and territories in urban areas. If one town runs out of suitable spaces, the animals move on to another instead of heading into the countryside. It's easy living.

Peregrine falcon nesting

High-rise life

Tall buildings, bridges, and other structures built by humans are surprisingly similar to rock faces, making them ideal as predator-free nesting sites for birds that would normally have a cliffside home. All around the globe, cliff dwellers, such as rock doves, have become city slickers. They are pursued by the world's fastest living animal—the peregrine falcon—which nests and roosts on the windowsils of high-rise apartment buildings. In coastal towns, herring gulls settle on factory and storehouse ledges, because they are a convenient substitute for the sea cliffs on which they would normally nest in the wild.

Swallows nesting on buildings

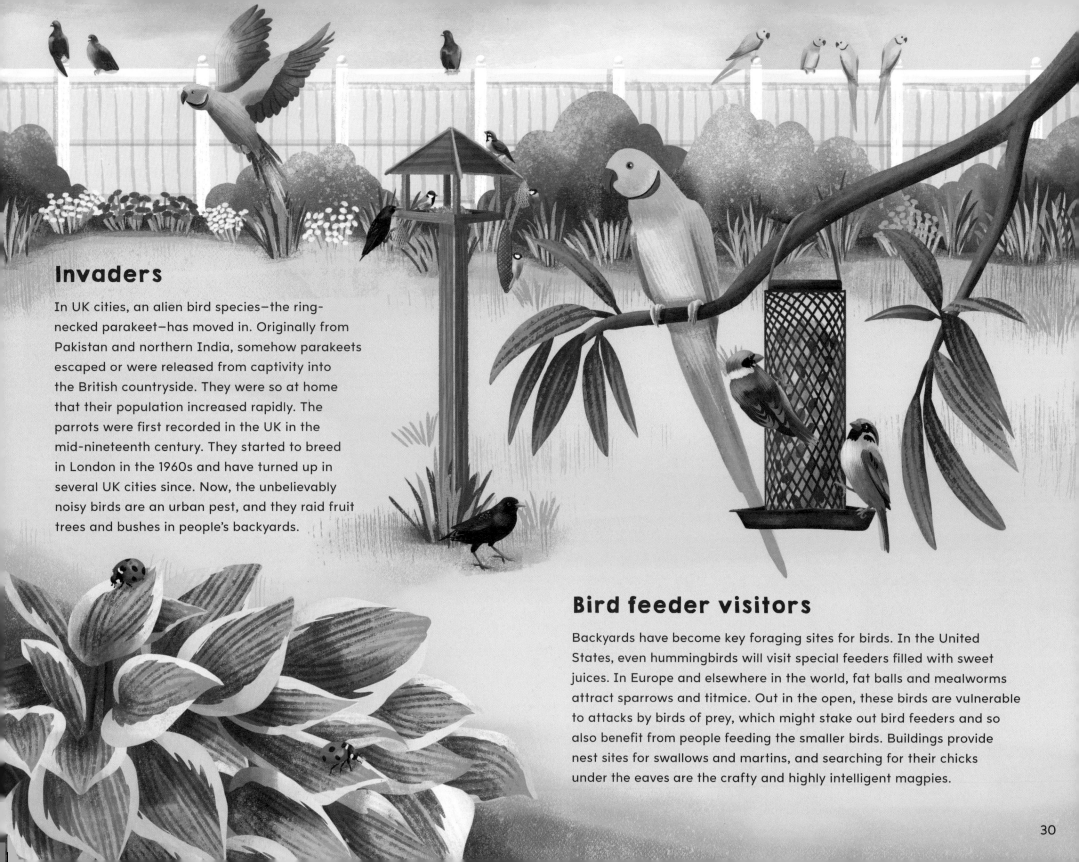

Invaders

In UK cities, an alien bird species—the ring-necked parakeet—has moved in. Originally from Pakistan and northern India, somehow parakeets escaped or were released from captivity into the British countryside. They were so at home that their population increased rapidly. The parrots were first recorded in the UK in the mid-nineteenth century. They started to breed in London in the 1960s and have turned up in several UK cities since. Now, the unbelievably noisy birds are an urban pest, and they raid fruit trees and bushes in people's backyards.

Bird feeder visitors

Backyards have become key foraging sites for birds. In the United States, even hummingbirds will visit special feeders filled with sweet juices. In Europe and elsewhere in the world, fat balls and mealworms attract sparrows and titmice. Out in the open, these birds are vulnerable to attacks by birds of prey, which might stake out bird feeders and so also benefit from people feeding the smaller birds. Buildings provide nest sites for swallows and martins, and searching for their chicks under the eaves are the crafty and highly intelligent magpies.